# St. Pope Kyrillos VI
## Holy Man of God

St. Mary & St. Demiana Convent

Saint Pope Kyrillos VI
Children's Saints Series
Copyright © 2023 St. Mary & St. Demiana Convent

All rights reserved.

Designed by the St. Mary & St. Demiana Convent
330 Village Drive
Dawsonville, GA 30534


Published by:
St. Mary & St. Moses Abbey Press
101 S Vista Dr., Sandia, TX 78383
stmabbeypress.com

All rights reserved. No part of this book may be reproduced or transmitted in any form or by any means without written permission from the author and publisher.

Illustrated by: Nancy Mikhael Barsoum
Written by: Mary Crocker

10 9 8 7 6 5 4 3 2

# Foreword

## "You are the light of the world."

~Matthew 5:14

As one body in Christ, our Church is united both in heaven and on earth. We who live here on this beautiful planet are well known by those who live up there in the Paradise of Joy, and every day they look out for us and talk to God on our behalf! So now it's our turn to get to know them! These saints—the Heroes of our Church and our great role models—are waiting to become our very best friends! As we get to know each one of them personally, we will not only gain companions for our everyday lives but also the best partners to walk with on the road to getting closer to our beloved Lord Jesus Christ.

With the blessing and prayers of our dear father, His Grace Bishop Youssef, it is with absolute great joy that we present the lives of the saints to you—the future generation of our Church!

May each new story learned be a flame used to light another's candle until the whole world is lit with the light of the glory of God in His saints!

May this be as great a blessing to you as it has been for us and may the intercessions of St. Mary, St. Pope Kyrillos VI, and the whole choir of angels and saints be with us all!

The story of Pope Kyrillos is about a holy man,

For whom God had a very great plan.

Early in life, he graduated and found a good job, too,

But he realized it wasn't what he wanted to do.

His family was not happy when he decided to quit,

But there was something special about him they had to admit.

He became a monk and what made him glad,

Was that the church named him Fr. Mina after the patron saint he had.

He was ordained a priest and went to the monastery,

But his heart wanted something out of the ordinary.

He loved to be with God and his dream to fulfill,

Was to be alone with God, so he moved to a windmill.

There he rose in the night to spend time with the Lord,

And keep company with the saints whom he had always adored.

But when Fr. Mina was called back to serve,

He packed up and obeyed without reserve.

Back at the church, he had a heart for the youth,

They came to him for prayer and spiritual truth.

Fr. Mina taught by words and by his example,

And the stories of the lives he touched are ample.

Fr. Mina's life was simple, and he was content,

But a life out of the spotlight was not God's intent.

For God needed a shepherd for His church to keep,

One who would love and guide His precious sheep.

A man of great prayer, faith and humility,

Not just a man would rely on his own ability.

Fr. Mina was nominated and ordained as the Pope,

And this gave the Church such a great hope.

God gave him gifts to prophesy and heal,

And he received all who came with an appeal.

Now something that many might have not realized,

Was the daily Eucharist, which the Pope greatly prized.

Pope Kyrillos's time saw spiritual transformation,

And in Zeitoun
St. Mary's apparition.

Over the years, tales of his miracles grew,

Stories told by young and old, believers and unbelievers, too.

Pope Kyrillos's goal in life wasn't to be grand,

He simply obeyed God's call and held His hand.

And like the Good Shepherd he sacrificed for his people, too,

Which teaches us what a life fully given over to God can do.

www.ingramcontent.com/pod-product-compliance
Lightning Source LLC
Chambersburg PA
CBHW041809040426
42449CB00001B/30